THE REVELATION AND THE
HISTORY OF CHRISTENDOM

T010566?

THE REVELATION
——AND——
THE HISTORY OF
CHRISTENDOM

Prophecy Fulfilled to the End of Our Time

VICTOR MCGOWAN

iUniverse, Inc.
Bloomington

The Revelation and the History of Christendom
Prophecy Fulfilled to the End of Our Time

iUniverse books may be ordered through booksellers or by contacting:

iUniverse
1663 Liberty Drive
Bloomington, IN 47403
www.iuniverse.com
1-800-Authors (1-800-288-4677)

ISBN: 978-1-4502-7809-6 (sc)
ISBN: 978-1-4502-7808-9 (ebk)

Printed in the United States of America

iUniverse rev. date: 12/23/2010

Who declared this Long ago,
Who declared it From the distant past?
Was it not I, the Lord?

Isaiah 45, 21

Contents

INTRODUCTION

Most of us reach a time in our lives when we wonder about the purpose of our existence. Are we only an accident of cosmic chemistry? Throughout history every society appealed to the gods for immortality from an intuitive belief that this life was s step toward an expanded existence. However, we live in a scientific age that prides itself in discounting the intuitive call to God that we sometimes sense. Perhaps various religions claim our loyalty, but we often accept a familial tradition. We are likely to say that we lack the intellectual evidence for God.

Fortunately, such evidence exists in the Revelation, the last book of the Bible. It will be shown to the careful reader that the prophecies of the Revelation have in fact been fulfilled during the last 1900 years of Christian history. Although the Revelation was given to Jesus' youngest apostle John in c.96 A.D., its full prophetic vision has been delayed until the events of the 20th century.

At this point, a skeptical reader may ask for evidence that it is possible that the Revelation's symbolism predicts history. The prophetic value of the Revelation was demonstrated in a book published in 1701 by Robert Fleming. (*The Rise and Fall of Rome Papal*).[1] The explanations given by Fleming for the symbols that identified previous historic events were similar to the explanations of Protestant reformers of the 16th and 17th centuries. They believed that the papacy was clearly identified in the Revelation's symbolic "prostitute" on the seven hills of Rome. (Rev. 17, 9, 15). Other identifications were also made to the rise of the Islamic religion. Fleming went beyond his own time, however, and made several guesses about the future based on the Revelation's symbols. These admitted guesses proved to be accurate when compared to major events of Christendom.

Fleming believed that the fourth vial, or bowl, of the Revelation poured out on the sun (Rev. 15, 8) concerned the French monarchy at the end of the 18th century, almost one hundred years into the future. "But as to the expiration of this vial, I do fear it will not be until 1794." The King of France, Louis XVI, was executed on January 21, 1793 during the French Revolution.

Fleming goes on to suppose that the next vial of the Revelation sequence foretells that "The fifth vial, (ver. 10, 11) which is to be poured out on the seat of the beast, or the dominions that more immediately belong to, and depend upon the Roman See [the Papal States of Italy]; that I say this judgment will probably begin in about the year 1794, and expire about 1848…. But we are not to imagine that this vial will totally destroy the papacy…." Those familiar with European history will remember that the French Revolution beginning in 1789 attacked the Roman Catholic Church. It also inspired

---

1   Fleming, Robert. *The Rise and Fall of Rome Papal*, 1701, reprinted from the 1848 2nd edition, 1987, H.V. Dorp.

many revolutions across Europe in 1848, including Italy and the Papal States, which were finally taken into the government of Italy in 1870, leaving only the Vatican grounds.

One more guess by Fleming makes it reasonable to believe that the Revelation signals historic events and eras. Fleming writes that "The sixth vial (ver. 12) will be poured out upon Mahometan Antichrist…. Supposing, then, that the Turkish monarchy should be totally destroyed between 1848 and 1900…." During this time the Turkish, Ottoman Empire lost significant territory, and it lost the remainder of its non-Turkish territory with the close of World War I. Within a few years, its new government of secular Turks caused the extinction of the Sultanate government and the religious Caliphate. Fleming's attempt to foresee the collapse of the Ottoman Empire as an event leading to a Muslim conversion to Christianity was mistaken. Nevertheless, using the Revelation's symbolic vials, Fleming did forecast the subject and general timing of the collapse of three great centers of power: the French Monarchy, the Papal States and the Ottoman Empire. Each of these had been serious obstacles to the progress of Christianity for hundreds of years, and their downfalls were among the most important events of history.

Most of the Protestant reformers of the 16th century, including Luther and Calvin, understood the Revelation as a mirror of history. Because much was not understood, however, the 19th century saw the revival of a theory that the entire Revelation was concerned only with the three years of a distant future, and it was to be understood in a very literal sense. This idea came from a Jesuit priest named Francisco de Ribera, who wrote his notes in 1585 A.D., to counter Protestants who saw the Papacy as the Antichrist, the one who stands in the place belonging to Christ. In 1841 A.D., the librarian of the Church of England discovered these notes, and published them as an academic matter. At this time, the urgency of the Reformation had declined, and the study of prophesy was set aside. Unfortunately, a leader of the Plymouth Brethren in Dublin, John Nelson Darby, accepted this view of futurism without realizing its Roman Catholic purpose.[2] Evangelical Christians today are persuaded to the futurist explanation without knowing the historic explanation. The latter has been published on a limited basis during the 20th century, but the futurist explanation has become popular with televangelists.

Mainline churches ignore the prophetic value of the Revelation, leaving the impression that they take the academic view that the Revelation is a 1st century pious fraud. This opinion reflects on the general lack of appreciation for a symbolic comparison with the important events of Christendom. The events of the 20th century however have greatly improved our understanding of the end-time symbols of the Revelation, leaving few doubts about its meaning.

The explanations given in this commentary are much the same as those given in the historical commentaries, some of which are noted as sources. Some key identifications are unique, however. It is hoped that they fill-in the gaps, or misunderstandings, of earlier efforts. The explanations of historical events are short, and mostly mirror commonly known circumstances of European history. The grand scenes of heaven and the theological aspects of the Revelation are left

---

2   The explanation concerning Ribera and Darby is given by Thomas Foster. *Amazing Book of Revelation Explained*!, 2nd edition, 1983.

to others. This commentary is largely limited to the historic progression of the Revelation's time-scale.

The physical scope of the Revelation is the territory of the Roman Empire at its greatest extent, as it was in John's day. At the beginning of the 2nd century, this territory included all the lands surrounding the Mediterranean Sea and most of Europe. However, it is not a world-wide view. It is the territory where Christianity developed for 1700 years – the "earth" of Christendom. The Revelation distinguishes between its Greek words for "earth" and "world", as in Rev. 13, 8.

John was in a visionary state when he was shown God's view of the future in shifting and fantastic images that cannot be fully understood in words. These dream-like images represent the quality of spiritual events rather than realistic scenes that can be easily visualized. Some parts of the text were dictated to him, such as the letters to the seven churches. In general, however John was writing from his impressions of his visionary experiences. These must be understood as metaphors, symbolic of the spiritual conditions of predicted historical events, not pictorial realities of historic scenes.

A caution must be offered to some readers who may be disturbed to realize that their beliefs are discordant with the explanations of the Revelation given here. If the explanation is correct, the author has no right to soften the words of God's text, or to modify historic facts. God foresees the course of history, but the evils that are noted in the Revelation are the work of humans pursuing their own ends without Him. His anger is the emotion of the Father of Creation, whose love cannot be indifferent to the rejection of salvation prepared by Jesus Christ, or the distortions of Christianity by erroneous leaders.

Messages to the Seven Churches – Rev. 2 & 3

The heavenly figure of Christ appeared to John the Apostle ca 96 A.D., when he was an old man and imprisoned by the Romans. Christ commanded John to write seven letters to seven churches in what is now western Turkey. Although the letters refer to the circumstances of these ancient churches, after 1900 years of Christian history, it is now clear that they also reveal the spiritual conditions of the major eras of Christianity:

1. the early era;
2. two centuries of martyrdom;
3. the triumphant imperial church;
4. ten centuries of Roman Catholic power;
5. the Protestant churches of the Reformation;
6. an era of evangelical enthusiasm, and
7. the modern age of indifference.

1.   Ephesus (to let go), 33 A.D. to ca. 116 A.D.

The first church included both Jewish and gentile believers. The letters of the New Testament describe the expectation of Christ's promised return in the near future. Disappointment certainly followed after the Roman army destroyed the Temple and killed tens of thousands of Jews in Jerusalem in 70 A.D. It is probable that many Christians fled from the approaching Roman army. This letter describes these Christians as loyal but disheartened.

Chapter 2, verse 1

Unto the church of Ephesus write

Verse 2

I know thy works, and thy labor and thy patience, and how thou canst bear them which are evil…

Verse 4

Nevertheless I have somewhat against thee, because thou hast left they first love.

Verse 5

Remember therefore from whence thou art fallen, and repent, and do the first works, or else I will come onto thee quickly, and will remove thy candlestick out of its place, except thou repent.

Verse 6

But this thou hast, that thou hatest the deeds of the Nicolaitans, which I also hate.

The early Jewish Christian church disappeared from the historic records after the 1st century. Their candlestick was removed, unlike all the remaining types of churches, which continued through Christian history. This disappearance of the early church was a predicted event.

The meaning of "Nicolaitans" in its Greek roots is "power over people". Paul the apostle sent a letter to the elders of the church of Ephesus ca. 60 A.D. which warns that evil people would attempt to be leaders in the church:

Acts 20, verse 29

> *For I know this, that after my departing shall grievous wolves enter in among you, not sparing the flock.*

Verse 30

> *Also of your own selves shall men arise, speaking perverse things, to draw away disciples after them.*

The validity of this letter as a predictive prophecy for this era also rests on the cumulative accuracy of the remaining letters.

2.   Smyrna (bitter anointing oil) ca. 117 to 313 A.D.

At the beginning of the 2nd century Bishop Ignatius of Antioch was condemned to execution in Rome. He wrote about his willingness to die and the need to separate Jewish traditions from Christian churches.[3] His letter is an appropriate indicator of the end of the first church era and the beginning of the second church era of martyrdom. At various times and places throughout the 2nd and 3rd centuries, Christians were arrested and executed, often in arenas by wild animals. In 303 A.D. the emperor gave an edict that resulted in ten years of the worst suffering, ending in 313 A.D., when Constantine became the first Christian emperor.

---

3   "Those, then, who lived by ancient practices arrived at a new hope. They ceased to keep the Sabbath and lived by the Lord's Day, on which our life as well as theirs shone forth…" *Early Christian Fathers*, ed. Cyril C. Richardson, The Westminster Press, Philadelphia, 1953, I, 96.

Revelation 2, verse 8

And unto the angel of the Church of Smyrna write: These things saith the first and the last, which was dead and is alive.

Verse 9

I know thy works and tribulation, and poverty. (but thou art rich) and I know the blasphemy of them which say they are Jews and are not, but are the synagogue of Satin.

As indicated by Bishop Ignatius' letter, Christians were urged to resist those who wanted to impose Jewish laws unto what had become a largely gentile church.

Verse 10

Fear none of those things which thou shalt suffer: behold, the devil shall cast some of you into prison, that ye may be tried; and ye shall have tribulation ten days: be thou faithful unto death, and I will give thee the crown of life.

In Biblical prophecy "days" are understood to mean "years". In both Isaiah (34:8) and Ezekiel (4:6) these prophets are told to count days as years. The ruthless application of this Roman edict from 303 A.D. to 313 A.D. is widely recognized as the culmination of the age of martyrdom in Roman history. Christ finds no fault with Christians of this era, in contrast with other church eras.

3. Pergamos (married to power) 313 A.D.

With the popularity of Christianity that followed Emperor Constantine's recognition and support of Christianity in 313 A. D., it became necessary to define the deity of Christ at a council of bishops in 326 A. D. During this council the key statement of what is known as the Trinity, or threefold expression of God as Father, Son and Spirit, was formalized as the Nicene Creed.[4] Many former pagans preferred to understand Jesus as a less than God, and the controversy was the subject of heated debates. Leading the supporters for the deity of Christ was a bishop named Athanasius of Alexandria. He insisted that one who was not fully God could neither reveal God nor give immortal life. He was banished by emperors five times, dying in 373 A.D., five years before the cause was won in 378 A.D. Without his heroic efforts Christianity would have failed. It seems reasonable to connect Athanasius to the name "Antipas" of the Revelation. This connection is supported by the Greek meaning of the name itself, "against all".

Chapter 2, verse 12

> *And to the angel in Pergamos write: These things saith he which hath the sharp sword with two edges.*

Verse 13

> *I know thy works, and where thou dwellest, even where Satan's seat is: and thou holdest fast my name, and has not denied my faith, even in those days wherein Antipas was my faithful martyr, who was slain among you, where Satan dwelleth.*

Though these verses obviously describe a situation and person in 96 A.D., they are symbolically appropriate to the third era: "Satan's seat" being the new Roman imperial city of Constantinople; and "Antipas" being Athanasius. The

---

4   For some Christians, the Trinity of God may be thought of as Creator Father, Savior Son and Companion Spirit. Three individual gods probably was not meant by the Greek word *persona* used in the creed. The same Greek word means the mask worn by an actor in a play. As fire may be understood as composing the attributes of flame, light and heat, so God may be understood as Father, Son and Spirit.

following verses also clarify the symbolic and historic identity of this church age.

Verse 14

> *But I have a few things against thee, because thou hast them that hold the doctrine of Balaam, who taught Balak to cast a stumbling block before the children of Israel, to eat things sacrificed unto idols, and to commit fornication.*

Balaam and Balak refer to an Old Testament incident in which Israelites were seduced into idolatry, which is commonly referred to as "fornication" in the Bible.[5] With the great influx of recent pagans into Christianity following Constantine's conversion, the practice of honoring martyrs with special days, feasts, depictions and amulets proved to be both popular and lucrative. These closely followed pagan rites and festivals. By the 6th century, there were celebrations for Mary that made no reference to Jesus, and he was frequently shown as an infant with Mary. The result of these practices was to distance many Christians from their God, even today.

Verse 15

> *So hast thou them that hold the doctrine of the Nicolaitans, which thing I hate.*

The 4th century saw the full development of the priest as one who stands between layperson and God, and who claims to be indispensable to the practice of Christianity. This is the belief of the Orthodox and Roman Catholic Churches. It is worthwhile at this point to remember the words of Jesus: "*But be not ye called Rabbi: for one is your Master, even Christ; and all ye are brethren. And call no man your father upon the earth:*

---

5   Numbers, Chapters 22 to 25, and Jeremiah, Chapters 3 and 6-10.

for one is your Father which is in heaven. Neither be ye called masters: for one is your Master, even Christ.[6]

4. Thyatira (continual incense), ca. 529 A.D.

The political realities of the Roman Empire, with its government relocated to Constantinople in 330 A.D., resulted in the gradual separation of the church into the Eastern Orthodox churches and the Western Roman Catholic Church. In 529 A.D. the Emperor Justinian confirmed papal supremacy in the Roman code of law. During the next thousand years, the Roman Catholic Church rose to great power and wealth throughout Europe, while the Eastern Orthodox churches lost much of their territory to the Muslim religion.

Verse 18

> *And unto the church in Thyatira write: These things saith the Son of God…*

Verse 19

> *I know thy works, and charity and service, and faith, and thy patience, and thy works; and the last to be more than the first.*

The most admirable activities of Roman Catholicism in the Middle Ages were the charitable works of monks, nuns, and inspired lay people. These works continue today, greater than in the past, as the wealth of societies has developed.

Verse 20

> *Notwithstanding I have a few things against thee, because thou sufferest that woman Jezebel, which calleth herself a prophetess, [one who speaks for God] to teach and seduce*

---

6   Matthew 23, verses 8-10.

my servants to commit fornication [idolatry] and to eat things sacrificed to idols [to make prayers to the dead].

The Popes and their hierarchy of priests encouraged and taught a form of Christianity laden with pagan practices. Like the Old Testament Jezebel who led Israelites to worship false gods, Roman Catholics were told to pray to saints, worship before relics, make pilgrimages to places declared holy, and believe that Popes were the representatives of Christ. During the thousand years of this era at its worst, the Popes conducted themselves disgracefully with every kind of crime. A full explanation of the history of Roman Catholicism is far beyond the scope of this brief commentary on the Revelation. Readers should be warned that many publications avoid a graphic portrayal of the papacy for the sake of acceptance by Roman Catholics.

Verse 21

And I gave her space [time] to repent of her fornication; and she repented not.

Verse 22

Behold, I will cast her into a bed, [a bed of suffering] and them that commit adultery with her into great tribulation, except they repent their deeds.

History bears witness to the loss of economic, political, and spiritual influence of the papacy in the last 500 years.

Verse 24

But unto you I say, and unto the rest in Thyatira, as many as have not this doctrine…I will put on you none other burden.

The average European of the Middle Ages lived a life with much solitude and suffering. They were formed in their personal prayers by their fears, pain, and hope in a Savior God felt rather than taught by priests.

Verse 25

But that which ye have already hold fast till I come.

The believers today are encouraged in this verse to endure in their faith in Christ, and they are distinguished here from those who continue to worship and follow the traditions sponsored by the Roman papacy.

5. Sardis (a semi-precious stone), ca. 1523 A.D.

At various times during the Middle Ages, brave people attempted to purify Christianity to no avail. Many were burned at the stake. Finally, Martin Luther nailed his famous complaints on a church door in 1517 A.D. Five years later, the Protestant movement gained momentum with the publication of the forbidden translations of the Bible. The churches that arose rejected the papacy and many of the practices of Roman Catholicism. Lutherans, Anabaptists, Presbyterians, Anglicans, and others returned to the authority of the Bible to reform their beliefs toward simplicity and personal responsibility for a Christ-centered life. Unfortunately, these churches chose to disagree over rather minor matters of doctrine. Most became attached to government control, and many lapsed into formulas of worship that lacked spiritual energy.

Chapter 3, verse 1

> *And unto the church in Sardis write; these things saith he that hath the seven spirits of God, and the seven stars; I know thy works, that thou hast a name that thou livest, and art dead.*

Verse 2

> *Be watchful and strengthen the things which remain, that are ready to die: for I have not found thy works perfect before God.*

Verse 3

> *Remember therefore how thou hast received and heard, and hold fast, and repent. If therefore thou shalt not watch, I will come as a thief, and thou shalt not know what hour I will come upon thee.*

The mainline Reformation churches of today have good reputations, but are often rather lifeless and "ready to die". They do not understand the Revelation, and they do not watch for the return of Christ with the urgency of belief.

Verse 4

> *Thou hast a few names even in Sardis which have not defiled their garments; and they shall walk with me in white; for they are worthy.*

Verse 5

> *He that overcometh, the same shall be clothed in white raiment; and I will not blot out his name out of the book of life, but I will confess his name before my father, and before his angels.*

That there are only "a few names" in the Sardis-era churches worthy of white garments is probably the result of believing that faith alone is sufficient for a Christian life. Recognition of Christ must be combined with a purified life.

6. Philadelphia (brotherly love), ca. 1739 A.D.

It comes as a welcome surprise that the church age following the deadly warfare and theological disagreements of the 16th and 17th centuries was an enthusiastic return to the original Christian experience of personal sinlessness and spiritual insight. This period, extending as a general movement into the 20th century, came to be called "the great awakening" by historians. It appealed especially to the poor and disenfranchised. It began with John Wesley who preached to Britain's working poor in a way that eventually resulted in the Methodist denomination.

Other denominations, such as Moravian, Baptist, and others also expanded the movement, often with large outdoor meetings. People attending these meetings felt themselves forgiven, healed, and blessed by the Spirit of God. The Biblical word was their authority, and all were told of their personal responsibility to seek God. These people upheld Jesus Christ through missionary societies, entering through an "open door", so to speak, to evangelize the world. This church age receives no criticism from Christ.

Chapter 3, verse 7

> *And to the angel of the church of Philadelphia write; These things saith he that is holy, he that is true, he that hath the key of David, he that openeth and no man shutteth; and shutteth, and no man openeth.*

Verse 8

> *I know thy works: behold I have set before thee an open door, no man can shut it: for thou hast a little strength, and hast kept my word, and hast not denied my name.*

Verse 9

> *Behold, I will make them of the synagogue of Satan, which say they are Jews, and are not, but do lie; behold I will make them to come and worship before thy feet, and to know that I have loved thee.*

A grave assault on Christianity began in 1820 when the Mormon religion was fabricated by Joseph Smith with a book of fantasy based on the belief that ancient Jews migrated to America. Recent DNA evidence exposes this as a lie. Their theology is rejected by all Christian churches. For example, they believe that Satan is the brother of Jesus, and that their god is one of countless other gods, each with a wife and a family, which is their destiny as Mormon believers.[7]

Verse 10

Because thou hast kept the word of my patience, I also will keep thee from the hour of temptation, which shall come upon all the world, to try them that dwell upon the earth.

There is hope in these lines that some Christians will not have to endure the end of the tribulation events.

7. Laodicea (power of the laity), ca. 1936 A.D.

Commentators on the current general state of Christianity note its lack of real enthusiasm, and its emphasis on the opinion of the individual. It is a common attitude that God conforms Himself to one's own opinions. For many Christians in the various denominations—Orthodox, Roman Catholic, Protestant, and Evangelical—there is a mood of indifference and comfortable participation in the modern life of self-absorption.

Chapter 3, verse 14

And unto the angel of the church of the Laodiceans write: These things saith the Amen, the faithful and true witness, the beginning of the creation of God.

Verse 15

I know thy works, that are neither cold nor hot: I would thou wert cold or hot. So then because thou art

---

7   "In Mormonism, Jesus is also seen as the brother of Satan. Since Satan was also a preexistent spirit creation of the male and female earth gods…. Jesus Christ is not unique…. His divinity is not unique, for every exalted man will attain the same Godhood…." John Ankerberg and John Weldon. *The Mormon Church*, Harvest House Publishers, Eugene, Oregon 97402, p. 19

lukewarm, and neither cold nor hot, I will spew thee out of my mouth.

Verse 17

Because thou sayest, I am rich and increased with goods, and have need of nothing; and knowest not that thou art wretched, and miserable, and poor, and blind, and naked:

Verse 18

I counsel thee to buy of me gold tried in the fire, that thou mayest be rich; and white raiment, that thou mayest be clothed, and that the shame of thy nakedness do not appear; and anoint thine eyes with eyesalve; that thou mayest see.

Verse 19

As many as I love, I rebuke and chasten: be zealous therefore, and repent.

Verse 20

Behold, I stand at the door, and knock: if any man hear my voice, and open the door, I will come in to him, and I will sup with him, and he with me.

Verse 21

To him that overcometh will I grant to sit with me in my throne, even as I overcame, and am set down with my Father in his thrown.

Verse 22

He that hath an ear, let him hear what the Spirit saith unto the churches.

There is no eighth church age. Accordingly, we may expect the promised return of Christ in our time. Robert Fleming, writing in 1701, who showed remarkable insight into the symbols and timing of the Revelation, guessed that Christ would return about 2017 A.D. This timing also coincides with the final prophetic statement of Daniel, as shown at the end of this commentary.

Another clue to the conclusion of our age may be deduced by the pairing of church eras: the first church's loss of love for Christ with the last church's lukewarm state. If a time line is drawn for the church eras, it forms a symmetry of years that may suggest the time of the return of Christ.

Church Eras

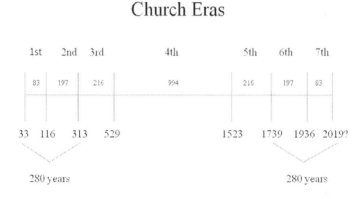

The odds of matching the actual and peculiar history of Christianity with the descriptions and sequential order of seven items occurring in a predetermined order are one in 5,040 (1x2x3x4x5x6x7). If details of these seven descriptions of the church eras are included in a calculation, the odds of this being the accident of a pious fraud rise to millions to one against coincidence.

THE SCROLL WITH
SEVEN SEALS

After the seven letters to the seven churches, we begin another portion of the Revelation devoted to future events affecting Christendom. We are given symbolic scenes that identify the timing of the progress of history during the tribulations of Christianity. These are the major political events that determine the circumstances that Christians must endure. Like stepping stones across the river of history, we are given just enough information to know that God is attentive to the woes of mankind.

We are told of a scroll, written on both sides, held by God, that is sealed with the seven seals. Only the Lord Jesus, described as the lion of the tribe of Judah, or a lamb sacrificed to redeem mankind, is allowed to open the seals. The seven seals lead on to another set of images called the seven trumpets, and finally to a third set of predictions called the seven vials. The overall timing of these historic eras can now be understood as follows:

Seven seals from 96 A.D. to 378 A.D.

Seven trumpets from 378 A.D. to 1517 A.D.

Seven vials from 1517 A.D. to the near future

First Seal – Roman conquests

Chapter 6, verse 1

> *And I saw when the Lamb opened one of the seals, and I heard, as it were the noise of thunder, one of the four beasts saying Come and see.*

Verse 2

> *And I saw and beheld a white horse: and he that sat on him had a bow; and a crown was given unto him: and he went forth conquering, and to conquer.*

At the time John saw this vision, the Roman Empire was reaching its maximum extent, encompassing all of the Mediterranean lands and much of Britain and Mesopotamia. Roman emperors and generals rode white horses. The Greek word for "crown" used here refers to the laurel leaf crown worn by Roman heroes, not the diadem of royalty worn by the returning Lord at the end of the Revelation. The first seal and its white horse represents the golden age of the Roman Empire from 96 A.D. to 164 A.D. at its maximum extent.

Second Seal – Roman civil wars

The second seal and its red horse represent the bloody age of warfare that continued for centuries of civil wars between rival emperors and wars with barbarian invaders.

Verse 3

> *And when he had opened the second seal, I heard the second beast say, Come and see.*

Verse 4

> *And there went out another horse that was red: and power was given to him that sat thereon to take peace from the earth, and that they should kill one another: and there was given unto him a great sword.*

Third Seal – Roman taxation

The third seal of the Roman decline, a black horse with a rider holding a pair of balances, represents the staggering increases in taxation demanded by the Rome for the support of the armies. In 212 A.D. the entire population of the empire, except slaves, was given the status of Roman citizens, making everyone liable to taxation. The shortage of coins made it necessary for the government to receive tax payments in grain and wine, which were subject to adulteration with dirt and water. Wages also were made in grain equivalents. Price controls were attempted at times. As much as 95 percent of taxes were made with payments of agricultural products.[8]

Verse 5

> *And when he had opened the third seal, I heard the third beast say, Come and see. And I beheld, and lo a black horse; and he that sat on him had a pair of balances in his hand.*

Verse 6

> *And I heard a voice in the midst of the four beasts say, a measure of wheat for a penny, and three measures of barley for a penny; and see thou hurt not the oil and wine [By adulteration]*

By the middle of the 3rd century, Roman emperors faced currency collapse, price inflation, and overwhelming attacks and losses on the upper Rhine and Danube. The upper middle class was almost taxed out of existence. The rural poor, of course, suffered the most. During the period from 185 to 284

---

8   Grant, Michael. *The Climax of Rome*, Weidenfeld, London, 1968, p. 61 and Chapter 3.

A.D., no less than 32 emperors seized the empire, and these in turn were opposed by 27 pretenders.

Fourth Seal – Deaths

Adding to this misery, the pale horse of death, the fourth seal, overshadowed the empire. The plague raged through the empire for 15 years from 250 to 265 A.D. "Famine is almost always followed by epidemical diseases, the effect of scanty and unwholesome food [and plague-bearing rats]…. During this time, five thousand persons died daily in Rome, and many towns that had escaped the hands of the barbarians were entirely depopulated."[9]

Verse 7

> *And when he had opened the fourth seal, I heard the voice of the fourth beast say, Come and see.*

Verse 8

> *And I looked, and beheld a pale horse: and his name that sat on him was Death, and Hell followed with him. And power was given unto them over the fourth part of the earth to kill with a sword, and with death, and with beasts of the earth.*

An estimate of 25 percent of the Roman world's population dying at this time is reasonable.

Fifth Seal – Martyrs

Following these images of the famous four horsemen of the Apocalypse, John was shown the fate of Christian martyrs—particularly those killed at the beginning of the 4th century, from 303 to 313 A.D., often by lions for amusement in amphitheaters.

---

9   Gibbon, Edward. *The Decline and Fall of the Roman Empire*, Chapter 10

Verse 9

> *And when he had opened the fifth seal, I saw under the altar the souls of them that were slain for the word of God, and for the testimony which they held:*

Verse 10

> *And they cried with a loud voice, saying How long, O Lord, holy and true, clost thou not judge and avenge our blood on them that dwell on the earth?*

Verse 11

> *And white robes were given to every one of them; and it was said unto them, that they should rest for a little season, until their fellow servants also and their brethren, that should be killed as they were, should be fulfilled.*

Sixth Seal – Rome becomes Christian

The sixth seal begins when Constantine the Great became the sole emperor from 324 to 337 A.D., and with him the Roman world was changed in its beliefs and its location. Constantine sheltered the Christian church. His mother had become a Christian in Britain, and he won his crucial battle in 313 A. D. after seeing a Christian symbol in the sky. Constantine took the government of Rome to the new city of Constantinople, today called Istanbul. Many saw the political advantages of becoming Christians, and the now-respectable church was swamped with people seeking power and position who had been devoted to pagan religions. The social and economic value of belonging to a pagan cult diminished. The sun, moon and stars, worshipped as homes of various pagan deities, had their shrines ignored or seized. The pagans who held political power were shaken and frightened for their positions. Mountains of power and islands of privilege were socially displaced. This time period was one of the greatest political and social upheavals of history.

Verse 12

> *And I beheld when he had opened the sixth seal, and lo, there was a great earthquake; and the sun became black as sackcloth of hair, and the moon became as blood;*

Verse 13

> *And the stars of heaven fell unto the earth, even as a fig tree casteh her untimely figs, when she is shaken of a mighty wind.*

Verse 14

> *And the heaven departed as a scroll when it is rolled together; and every mountain and island moved out of their places.*

The pagan religion most affected by Christianity in some of its ceremonies was Mythricism. Its ceremonies were conducted in caves, actual or artificial, and it drew its believers from all social ranks, unusual for a pagan religion. It was very popular, highly secretive, and particularly valued by the military. Of course they prayed for the mountains of power to fall unto them, not the Christians. Knowing of the belief of Christians that Christ would return, they feared a wrathful God.

Verse 15

> *And the kings of the earth, and the great men, and the rich men, and the chief captains, and the mighty men, and every bondsmen, and every free man, hid themselves in dens and in the rocks of mountains:*

Verse 16

> *And said to the mountains and rocks, Fall on us, and hide us from the face of him that sitteth on the throne, and from the wrath of the Lamb:*

Verse 17

> *For the great day of his wrath is come; and who shall be able to stand?*

The emperor Julian, who had been a Christian in his youth, briefly revived the pagan cults. His death in 363 A.D. was the last hope of many pagans for a revival of their religion and status. A massive earthquake occurred in 364 A.D. in the Eastern Mediterranean Sea, which gives this era an earthly reality that underscores its prophetic symbolism.[10] For the next 200 years, there were many more large earthquakes than usual for this area, occurring at a time when the Roman world was also shaken politically by the barbarian invasions beginning in 378 A.D., when the seventh seal of seven trumpets begins.

All historians would agree with the sequence of major events of the Roman Empire signified by the seven seals, as understood here. The first seal and its white horse of conquest and control reaching its greatest extent under Trajan (98-117 A.D.), who added northern Arabia, Armenia, Mesopotamia and Dacia (Hungary) to the empire. The revolt of the Jews under their false messiah Barkochba from 131 to 135 A.D. was followed by other internal wars from 162 to 211 A.D. This revolt and the internal wars were the red horse of war and the second seal. Taxation and a barter economy are signified by the black horse of the third seal, followed by the pale, fourth horse of a period of great mortality by plague (250-265 A.D.) and famine. The fifth seal of martyrdom for ten years (303-313 A.D.) and the sixth seal of Constantine's removal of

---

10   Gore, Rick. *"Wrath of Gods, Centuries of Upheaval Along the Anatolian Fault", National Geographic,* July 2000. Massive quakes occurred in 364, 458, 526 and 588 A.D. Ephesus, Smyrna, Pergamon and Antioch were among the destroyed cities.

government to Constantinople complete the symbolism to 378 A.D., when the seventh seal reveals the first trumpet.

Chapter 7 of the Revelation is a retrospective chapter inserted between the historic series of the six seals and the next historic sequence of the seven trumpets. Chapter 7 concerns the fate of 144,000 witnesses and a great multitude of people whose lives have been cleansed to salvation by the Lord's sacrificial death. These are the Christians who suffered for their faith during the early centuries of Christianity.

SEVENTH SEAL OF SEVEN TRUMPETS

Proceeding directly to Chapter 8, the seventh seal is now opened, and it consists of seven angels blowing seven trumpets of judgment, beginning in 378 A.D. to 1517 A.D., when the last trumpet sounds. Each of these trumpet eras greatly stressed the people of Christ, who often paid for their loyalty in duress and blood.

After the struggles within the church to continue to recognize the deity of the Son of God, a second source of destruction to Christianity came in the religion of barbarian invaders of the Roman Empire. They had been taught a form of Christianity called Arianism that did not grasp the significance of God conjoined with mankind by Jesus Christ. To them, Christ was merely an extraordinary man, not himself of God.

First Trumpet – Visigoths

The first trumpet sounded when the declining Roman Empire suffered a grave defeat in 378 A.D. In that year, the northern third of the Roman earth was lost in battle to the

Visigoths, who stormed through the grasslands of Hungary and the forests of Western Europe as well as the cities of Greece, Italy and France. These barbarian invaders came from southern Russia and were followed by many other tribes that eventually became the people of much of Europe.[11] Most of them believed in the Arian version of Christianity, with the exception of the powerful Franks, who became Roman Catholics.

Chapter 8, Verse 7

> *The first angel sounded, and there followed hail and fire mingled with blood, and they were cast upon the earth: and the third part of trees was burnt up, and all green grass was burnt up.*

The "third part" refers to the northern European third of the Roman Empire.

Second Trumpet – Vandals

Following the Visigoths a second wave of barbarians swept across Europe, announced in the Revelation as the second trumpet. These were the Vandals, who also were fleeing westward to escape the advancing Huns. The Vandals also invaded Italy, and eventually stopped in Spain. After learning how to construct and sail ships, they invaded the Roman world of northern Africa, Rome's breadbasket, in 427 A.D. In spite of their semi-Christian, Arian religion, they brutally ruled over the Christian population. Their ships controlled the Western Mediterranean Sea and the African coast—one-third of the Roman Empire.

---

11   Wallace, Hadrill, J.M. *The Barbarian West: The Early Middle Ages*, Harper Torchbooks, 1962, p. 21. The West Germans were Franks, Alamans, Saxons, Frisians, and Thuringians. The East Germans, east of the Oder River, were Goths, Vandals, Gepids and Lombards. The Scandinavians never migrated.

Verse 8

And the second angel sounded, and as it were a great mountain burning with fire was cast into the sea: and a third part of the sea became blood;

Verse 9

And the third part of ships were destroyed.

Third Trumpet – Huns

In the middle of the 5th century, when the third trumpet sounds, Attila the Hun fell upon the upper third of the Roman Empire, where many of Europe's rivers begin, including the Danube and Rhine. He was finally defeated in 451 A.D. in northwestern France by the Roman and Visigoth army.

Verse 10

And the third angel sounded, and there fell a great star from heaven, burning as it were a lamp, and it fell on the third part of the rivers, and upon the fountains of waters;

Verse 11

And the name of the star is called Wormwood; and a third part of the waters became wormwood, and many men died of the waters, because they were made bitter.

A falling star is associated in the Bible with the downfall of an evil ruler.[12]

Fourth Trumpet – Sun darkens

The fourth trumpet period begins in 535 A.D. with an astonishing historical event, well documented by eyewitnesses. The sun lost much of its light for 18 months. It is now

---

12   Isaiah 14:12. "How art thou fallen from heaven, O Lucifer…."

understood that a huge volcanic eruption in Indonesia was the cause of this catastrophic event.[13] Among five historical sources, the Roman official and historian Procopius is typical: "And it came about this year that a most dread portent took place. For the sun gave forth its light without brightnesses like the moon during this whole year, and it seemed exceedingly like the sun in eclipse, for the beams it shed were not clear, nor such as it is accustomed to shed." The volcanic dust also caused the moon and stars to become pale. There were crop failures over the entire earth, and temperatures fell to their lowest levels in 2,000 years.[14]

Verse 12

> *And the fourth angel sounded, and the third part of the sun was smitten, and the third part of the moon, and the third part of the stars; so as the third part of them was darkened, and the day shone not for a third part of it, and the night likewise.*

Procopius also wrote that "from the time this thing happened, men were not free from war, nor pestilence, nor anything leading to death." The centuries from the middle of the 6th century onwards are called the Dark Ages by historians, who note the decline of knowledge, religion, and the economy of Western Europe. A thousand years pass in the Revelation prophecy at this point before there are any more references to European Christendom. These centuries are the era of Roman Catholic Christianity: the time of the fourth church of Thyatira and the distortions of this church age by the papacy.

---

13   Keys, David. *Catastrophe*, Ballantine Books, 1999.
14   *Ibid.*, Appendix

Fifth Trumpet – Muhammed's conquests

The fifth trumpet sounded in 610 A.D. when a Satanic vision descended upon a confused Muhammed. The Koran soon followed, as did the conquests that removed one-third of mankind from the knowledge of Christ. The Muslim religion followed the Arab armies from 622 A.D. to 1057 A.D., when Turkish Muslims gradually took control of most of North Africa and the Middle East. The Greek Christianity of the Eastern Roman Empire was greatly reduced in size and the Empire ended when Constantinople was lost in 1453 A.D.

The Revelation identifies the times of the Arab and Turkish assaults on Christianity as the first and second "woes."

Verse 13

And I beheld, and heard an angel flying through the midst of heaven, saying with a loud voice, Woe, woe, woe to the inhabiters of the earth by reason of the other voices of the trumpet of the three angels, which are yet to sound.

Chapter 9, verse 1

And the fifth angel sounded, and I saw a star fall from heaven unto the earth: and to him was given the key of the bottomless pit.

The identity of the falling star symbol may be understood from Jesus' words when he said, "I beheld Satan as lightning fall from heaven" (Luke 10, verse 18).

Verse 2

And he opened the bottomless pit, and there arose a smoke out of the pit, as the smoke of a great furnace; and the sun and air were darkened by reason of the smoke of the pit.

Readers of Muhammed's Koran know the smoke of confusion rising from its words, and its dark claim to reveal a God of blood and oppression, distant from mankind.

Verse 3

> *And there came out of the smoke locusts upon the earth; and onto them was given power, as the scorpions of the earth have power.*

The locust swarms that occur in the Middle East often arise from the Arabian Desert, as did the Muslim Arabs who conquered in the years following Mohammed's death in 632 A.D.

Verse 4

> *And it was commanded them that they should not hurt the grass of the earth, neither any green thing, neither any tree; but only those men which have not the seal of God in their foreheads.*

Muslim armies were unusual for that age because their religion forbade them to destroy the crops or trees of their enemies. They were also instructed not to harm Christians they conquered because the Christians honored the Old Testament. Slaves in those times might be branded on their foreheads, but the reference here is to Christians who were servants of Christ in their minds.

Verse 5

> *And to them it was given that they should not kill them, but that they should be tormented five months: and their torment was as the torment of the scorpion, when he striketh a man.*

Five months, or 150 days, are counted as years in Biblical prophecy. There are 150 years from 632 A.D. when Muhammed died and his followers swept across Asia and Africa to 782 A.D., when a truce was purchased by the east Roman Empire.

Gradually this empire, known as Byzantium, regained its defensive capabilities in the centuries that followed. The Muslim authorities allowed Christians their religion, but treated them as inferiors, idolaters who had to pay high taxes. This policy had the effect of causing weak Christians to become Muslims. Stinging insults were aimed at Christians.

Verse 6

> *And in those days shall men seek death, and shall not find it; and shall desire to die, and death shall flee from them.*

The Muslim religious quest to die fighting for Islam and go to paradise was not the fate of most Muslim warriors, whose superiority of numbers, armor, and spirit overwhelmed their opponents.

Verse 7

> *And the shapes of the locusts were like unto horses prepared unto battle; and unto their heads were as it were crowns like gold, and their faces were as the faces of men.*

At this point John's vision of locusts transforms into a realistic glimpse of actual Muslim armies with their unique chainmail and painted metal helmets over their long hair.

Verse 11

> *And they had a king over them, which is the angel of the bottomless pit, whose name in the Hebrew tongue is Abaddon, but in the Greek tongue hath his name Apollyon.*

The names mean "destruction" and "Destroyer," again linking Islam to Satan.

Verse 12

> *One woe is past, and behold, there come two woes more hereafter.*

Sixth Trumpet – Turkish horsemen

Verse 13

> *And the sixth angel sounded, and I heard a voice from the four horns of the golden altar which is before God.*

Verse 14

> *Saying to the sixth angel which had the trumpet, Loose the four angels which are bound in the great river Euphrates.*

The headwaters of the Euphrates River in Turkey gave the Byzantine Empire its eastern boundary against Muslim attacks. In the 11th century the Byzantine Empire included most of Turkey, the Balkans and Greece. All of this territory was eventually lost. This loss of one-third of existing Christendom to the Turkish peoples was the sixth trumpet. These Turkish people of several races originated in northern Asia, and they believed it was their destiny to conquer the vast area under their endless sky, spoken by them as the four directions, or corners of the earth. The Revelation correctly treats these people as one, though they came as Seljuk, Mongol and Ottoman conquerors.

The first wave of Turkish assaults took place in 1055 A.D., when the Seljuks took peaceful control of Bagdad, the magnificent city of the Arab Caliphate. The Caliph was the person who represented the political, economic and religious heart of Islam. After consolidating their control of Bagdad, the Seljuks began to assault the territory of Byzantium, including Arzeroum at the headwaters of the Euphrates River. "The myriads of Turkish horse overspread a frontier of six hundred miles from Tauris to Arzeroum, and the blood of one hundred and thirty thousand Christians was a grateful sacrifice to the Arabian prophet." [15] This assault was likely to have begun in

---

15   Gibbon. Vol. 6, chapter LVII

1057 A.D., eventually resulting in the Turkish conquest of Constantinople and Byzantium in 1453 A.D., 396 years later.

Verse 15

> *And the four angels loosed, which were prepared for an hour, and a day, and a month, and a year, for to slay the third part of men.*

Following the Biblical meaning, we add one day, 30 days, and 365 days to a total of 396, understood as years, just as it happened in fact from 1057 A.D. to 1453 A.D. when the Ottoman Turks defeated the Greeks defending Constantinople.

Verse 16

> *And the numbers of the army of horsemen were two hundred thousand thousand: and I heard the number of them.*

The Greek meaning of the word "myriad" could be understood as either "thousand" as in the King James translation given here, or "ten thousand." The Greek means myriads of myriads. The Turkish and Mongol peoples organized their cavalry on units of ten, hundred, and thousand. What is meant here is 200 thousand horsemen, in units of thousands, just as became the historical fact over the time of these conquests.[16]

Verse 17

> *And thus I saw the horses in the vision, and them that sat on them, having breastplates of fire, and of jacinth, and brimstone: and the heads of the horses were as the heads of lions, and out of their mouths issued fire and smoke and brimstone.*

---

16 Many recent commentators misunderstand this meaning and teach it as 200 million. This is impossible. If "myriad" is 10,000, then 200 x 10,000 equals 2 million horsemen organized in units of 10,000 – a possibility.

Even today, the horsemen of Mongolia wear red, blue and yellow during celebrations of their skills. When the Ottoman Turks finally captured the great walled city of Constantinople, they used cannons with gunpowder, an early use in warfare. Some of these cannons were cast with lion's head muzzles that certainly must have roared like lions. They may be seen today in Istanbul.

Verse 19

> *For their power is in their mouth, and in their tails, for their tails were like onto serpents, and had heads, and with them they do hurt.*

The Turkish and Mongolian armies had leaders that announced their status to the world by the number of horsetails hung from a standard. These men administered the captured lands with ruthless efficiency. The importance of these horsetail standards may be seen today on the sultan's standard in a museum in Istanbul.

Verse 20

> *And the rest of the men which were not killed by these plagues yet repented not of the works of their hands, that they should not worship devils, and idols of gold, and silver, and brass, and of wood; which neither can see, nor hear, nor walk:*

Verse 21

> *Neither repented they of their murders, nor of their sorceries, nor of their fornication, nor of their thefts.*

An overall view of Christianity of the Middle Ages is disturbing because of the devotion of the churches—Eastern Orthodox and Western Roman—to icons, statuary, relics, saints, priests, and Popes. The loose political organization of kingdoms known as the Holy Roman Empire, coupled with the papacy, dictated the lives of most of the population of Western Europe. The Revelation has several chapters devoted to these circumstances before continuing the historical timeline with the pouring out of the seven vials. These chapters will be explained following the seven vials.

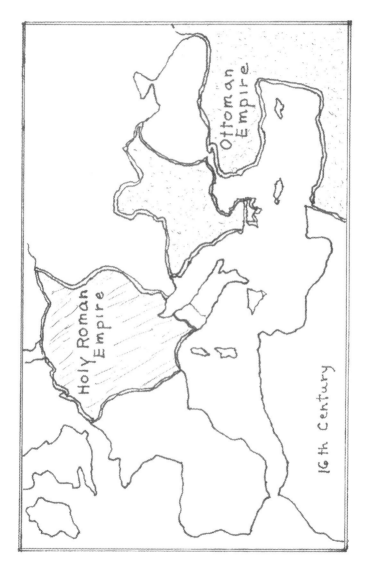

"The Holy Roman and Ottoman Empires around 1550 A.D."

The Seven Vials

At this point, we will continue with the historic time-scale of the Revelation by explaining the probable meaning of the seven vials (bowls). We will return later to the chapters between the sixth trumpet and the first vial. The seven vials signal the time from the 16th century through the 20th century. These vials are subtle clues to the timing of these last prophecies, and are not so easily recognized as the churches, seals, and trumpet eras. The vials are signal events of history that locate the spiritual condition of that era on a historic time-scale. They are not the cause of the historic events, or eras. The spiritual failures of Christendom belong to man, not God. The vials are poured out as the results that follow the evils chosen by mankind.

First Vial – Syphilus
Chapter 16, verse 1

> *And I heard a great voice out of the temple saying to the seven angels, Go your ways, and pour out the vials of the wrath of God upon the earth.*

Verse 2

> *And the first went and poured out his vial upon the earth;*
> *and there fell a noisome and grievous sore upon the men*
> *which had the mark of the beast, and upon them which*
> *worshipped his image.*

In John's day, some slaves were marked on their foreheads and hands by their owners. The Biblical sense used here is extended to the governments of the Middle Ages. It is especially applicable to the Germanic aristocracy of the Holy Roman Empire, with their papal support for the claim to a divine right to rule. This identification of the "beast" as the Holy Roman Empire follows from the prophecy of Daniel.[17] The worshipped image is the papacy.

The sores featured here place the first vial at that great turning point of Christian history, the beginning of the 16th

---

17   Daniel, Chapter 7, verse 7: "After this I saw in the night visions, and behold a fourth beast, dreadful and strong exceedingly; and it had great iron teeth: it devoured and broke in pieces, and stamped the residue with the feet of it: and it was diverse from all the beasts that were before it; and it had ten horns." The first beast, like a lion given a heart, whose (American) wings are torn off, refers to the British people. The second beast, like a bear, is the Slavic people. The third beast, like a leopard with four heads, is the people of the Atlantic Coast—Netherlands, France, Spain and Portugal. All arose in the sixth century and slowly became the great empires of the 16th Century. The Little Horn (Verses 8, 20-25) comes to power after the ten-horned Barbarian governments. It represents the papacy, ruling with the seven-horned electoral beast of the Holy Roman Empire. The three-horns removed are the Arian Vandals and Burgundians – both defeated in 535 A.D. – and the Ostrogoths in 553 A.D.. The Little Horn of the papacy will oppress the "saints" for 3 ½ times—1260 Biblical years—probably from the 756 A.D. defeat of the Lombards by the Franks and the resultant independence of the papacy to ca. 2016 A.D.

century. It was then that Columbus' crew returned carrying syphilis, which swept through Europe and beyond in a few years. The disease spreads by sexual contact, and therefore infected the least moral people, whatever their social position, including popes and kings. The second stage of the disease shows itself as a skin rash, which people attempted to treat with mercury vapors and arsenic powder. Incidentally, this use of mercury and arsenic led to the popularity of wigs to replace hair lost to mercury. The 16th century was the starting point for the pouring out of this vial on a notably immoral century. The fear of contracting syphilis helped to cause a considerable reduction in casual sexual behavior for the next 450 years.

Second Vial – Muslims control the Mediterranean Sea
Verse 3

And the second angel poured out his vial upon the sea; and it became as the blood of a dead man: and every living soul died in the sea.

The "sea" refers to the "sea of mankind", and the spiritual death of Europe that extended into the 18th century. The historic event that signals the time of this spiritual vision is the famous naval battle of Protestant Britain with Catholic Spain, and the final defeat of the huge Spanish armada in 1588. Had Spain been successful, it is likely that the Protestant cause would have failed. Equally appropriate, as a signal event of the time, was the huge sea battle of Lepanto in 1571 in the eastern Mediterranean between Christians (Spain, Venice, and the Papal States) and the Muslim Turks. Eventually, the Ottomans retained control of the Mediterranean Sea, but it was a continuous brawl for many years consuming thousands of lives.

It must be understood that John's visions were not seen as the actual historic events; rather, they must have been dreamlike images. His description of "every living soul" is an impression, not a literal fact.

Third Vial – Thirty Years War

Verse 4

> *And the third angel poured out his vial upon the rivers and fountains of waters, and they became blood.*

This verse signifies the time of the terrible devastation of the Thirty Years' War, ending in 1648 with one-third of northern Europe's population dead. In general, it was a war of religion between Catholic and Protestant princes, centered on the rivers flowing out of the Alps. Biblical symbols of streams and fountains of water are often used as poetic references to the outpouring of God's blessings. In this era, men used religion to pour out blood. The population of Germany fell from 17 million in 1618 to 8 million in 1648 due to war, famine and disease. The outcome of this brutal war gave permanence to the Protestant territories.

Verse 5

> *And I heard the angel of the waters say, Thou art righteous, O Lord, which art and wast, and shall be, because thou hast judged thus.*

Verse 6

> *For they have shed the blood of saints and prophets, and now hast given them blood to drink; for they are worthy.*

Verse 7

> *And I heard another out of the altar say, Even so, Lord God Almighty, true and righteous are thy judgments.*

It should be remembered here that the papacy promoted by trials of torture and by warfare the death of tens of thousands of Christians over six centuries. This bloody history is downplayed in many modern texts.

Fourth Vial – Sun King, Louis XIV to Napoleon
Verse 8

> *And the fourth angel poured out his vial upon the sun; and power was given unto him to scorch man with fire.*

Louis XIV, King of France from 1654 to 1715, was known as the "sun king" for the luxury of his lifestyle and his autocratic powers. He conducted four wars attempting to enlarge his boundaries. The power and style of the French monarchy extended to the execution of Louis XVI in 1793 during the French revolution. Under General Napoleon, the French "sun" scorched much of Europe from Spain to Russia in vast battles of conquest before his final defeat in 1815.

Verse 9

> *And men were scorched with great heat, and blasphemed the name of God, which hath power over these plagues: and they repented not to give him glory.*

The 18th century is called the "Enlightenment" because the intellectual class of men abandoned Jesus Christ, the intimate God, for a concept of an impersonal and distant power. This philosophy of "deism" was taken to its logical end during the French Revolution, when many believed that men should be ruled by "reason," the god of man himself.

Fifth Vial – Papal darkness

Verse 10

> *And the fifth angel poured out his vial upon the seat of the beast; and his kingdom was full of darkness; and they gnawed their tongues for pain.*

Verse 11

> *And blasphemed the God of heaven because of their pains and their sores, and repented not of their deeds.*

The "seat of the beast" refers to the Papal States of central Italy. This vial encompasses the time period from 1806 to 1870. During much of this time, the papacy was fighting off insurrections within its borders. These rebels were called *Carbonari*—charcoal burners, men hidden by the smoke of secrecy – an astonishing identification with the "darkness" surrounding the papacy.

The beast of Revelation is the same beast introduced in the prophecy of Daniel, Chapter 7. This beast is the symbolic representation of the Holy Roman Empire with its ten electoral heads, which were later reduced to seven electors, who chose the emperor. This form of feudal government supported the European aristocracy and its oppression of the common man for over 1,000 years. This "beast" took the place of the "dragon" of the Roman Empire. The Popes used the kingdoms of Europe to uphold its ownership of central Italy by claiming to represent God as the necessary agent to "anoint" the emperor's holy, civil authority. These are the "beast" and the papal "woman" who rides the beast, mentioned in other parts of the Revelation.

The Holy Roman Empire collapsed under the armies of Napoleon in 1806. The Pope was humiliated by Napoleon, who took the ceremonial crown from the Pope and placed it on his own head, effectively denying the need for civil government to seek the papacy for legitimacy. The papacy became irrelevant to European politics and the Papal States were taken into the Italian nation in 1870. The Pope issued the Christ-challenging doctrines of the virginal conception of Mary in 1848, and of papal inerrancy in 1870. Such was the "gnawing" of their tongues.

Sixth Vial – Three frogs of Nietzsche, Marx and Darwin

Verse 12

> *And the sixth angel poured his vial upon the great river Euphrates; and the water thereof was dried up, that the way of the kings of the east might be prepared.*

This reference to the drying up of the Euphrates River comes from the biblical account of the conquest of ancient Babylon in 539 B.C., when the Euphrates was diverted to allow an army to enter Babylon (Daniel, Chapter 5). It will be recalled that the Turkish Muslims began their assault on the Christian Byzantine Empire on the Euphrates in 1057 A.D. The Turks also took over the Egyptian Muslim caliphate that extended through North Africa in 1517 to complete their control of the eastern Mediterranean world. The Turkish empires held the Euphrates and much of the old Roman Empire from 1057 A.D. to 1918 A.D., when the Ottomans were defeated in World War I. The drying up of the Euphrates means the loss of military strength at this time. The negotiations following the war reduced Turkey to its present size and divided up the Middle East into the nations we know today as Syria, Palestine, Jordan, Iraq, Saudi Arabia, Kuwait and others, including (by influence) Iran. These nations, or "kings of the east," are playing out their historic role today, preparing for the destruction of Israel.

Verse 13

> *And I saw three unclean spirits like frogs come out of the*
> *mouth of the dragon, and out of the mouth of the beast,*
> *and out of the mouth of the false prophet.*

Toward the end of the 19th century, three major ideas developed in Europe from the theories of Friedrich Nietzsche, Karl Marx and Charles Darwin. These theories lay beneath the political movements of fascism, communism and racism that most attracted the people who lived in the territory that was once the Holy Roman Empire—modern Germany and Italy.

In Italy, Benito Mussolini rose to dictatorial power proclaiming the personal superiority of some men, popularized from the philosophy of Nietzsche. This aspect of fascism reflects the ancient Roman emperors' claims to be gods, and derives its name from the old Roman symbol for imperial power. The Revelation and Daniel recognize the old Roman Empire as a "dragon" that precedes the "beast" of the Holy Roman Empire.

In Germany, the communism promoted by the writings of Karl Marx took hold after World War I in a bloody competition with the fascism of Adolph Hitler. The "beast" of the prophecies, the Holy Roman Empire of German ambition, found new life in Hitler's claim to a third *Reich* (empire). It was Hitler's desire to crush the popular workers' movement of communism, which opposed him. That motivated the Pope to silence Catholic workers' opposition to Hitler because the Pope feared communist intentions for the Catholic Church.

Behind the racist murders by Hitler's Nazis of Jews and Slavic people lay the belief that warfare was a matter of the survival of the fittest—a genetic battle for superiority. Capitalism, too, shared this undercurrent of thinking that led to the brutal working conditions that inspired communism. These political events are distortions, of course, of the theories of Nietzsche, Marx, and Darwin, who became the prophet of science and the modern belief in the accidental creation of life. The wondrous creation of God became an accident of nature for many people. The Revelation uses the term "false prophet" in the sense of one who speaks in the place of God. With eager passion, the prophets of science promote the belief that chemical accidents have replaced the God of creation, with the result that science has now the religious significance of atheism. Many scientists use the scientific facts concerning substance to promote a religion of creation by "Nature."

Verse 14

> *For they are the spirits of devils working miracles, which go forth onto the kings of the earth and the whole world, to gather them to the battle of that great day of God Almighty.*

Verse 15

> *Behold, I come as a thief, Blessed is he that watcheth, and keep his garments, lest he walk naked, and they see his shame.*

There will not be a supernatural announcement of some kind when the Lord returns for his people. Those who expect some sort of warning period will not be ready for Him. We are warned here that this world war is not the time of Christ's return.

Verse 16

> *And he gathered them together into a place called in Hebrew tongue Armageddon.*

The Megiddo valley of Israel saw many ancient battles, but its similar sounding "Armageddon" is symbolic of a great battlefield, not of a location in Israel, but of a scene of great warfare. "Armageddon" is commonly used with reference to World War II in the popular media.

Seventh Vial – World War II

Verse 17

> *And the seventh angel poured out his vial into the air, and there came a great voice out of the temple from the throne, saying, It is done.*

Verse 18

> *And there were voices and thunders and lightnings; and there was a great earthquake, such as was not since men were upon the earth, so mighty an earthquake, and so great.*

No wars in history approach the scale of death and destruction of the "earthquake" of World War II and its 45 million deaths. For the first time in history, a war was fought in the air.

Verse 19

> *And the great city was divided into three parts, and the cities of the nations fell: and great Babylon came in remembrance before God, to give unto her the cup of the wine of the fierceness of his warmth.*

"Babylon" is the word used in Revelation to identify the spiritual condition of nations opposed to God.

Verse 20

> *And every island fled away, and the mountains were not found.*

During World War II, Europe was divided into three parts: Italian, German, and Russian areas of control. The Bible uses the "islands" and "mountains" to mean small and large nations, or governments, and World War II certainly reorganized Europe.

Verse 21

> *And there fell upon men a great hail out of heaven, every stone about the weight of a talent: and men blasphemed God because of the plague of the hail; for the plague was exceedingly great.*

The destruction of German cities during World War II is often shown in newsreels today. Bombs did much of the damage, but the greatest killing weapons were massed artillery barrages with shells weighing about 60 pounds, the weight of a biblical talent. Since World War II, Europeans express their irreverent attitude toward God by their indifference for Christian worship. Their churches are empty.

This discussion ends the successive progress of the Revelation through the spiritual history of Christianity, using the seven church eras, seven seals, seven trumpets, and seven vials as our guide. We are not given any more historical information up to our current time. However, more scenes follow at the end of Revelation that apply to the future—either on earth or in heaven.

The few remaining chapters of the Revelation are in our future, and are close upon us. We are told of a rider on a white horse in heaven, with a robe dipped in blood, whose name is the Word of God and Lord of Lords. There is a final battle of kings of the earth against the Lord and His celestial army. There is much to debate in these final chapters that has theological significance. The gathering of the elect, the final battle, the thousand years that follow, and the final judgment are beyond this historical review.

Neither selection of historic events nor random chance can account for the pairing of the Revelation verses with the major circumstances of Christendom. That events and verses also occur in the same sequential order is evidence for God in Christ beyond any reasonable doubt. More evidence for the historic accuracy of the Revelation is found in the chapters that are aside from the time-line chapters of the seals, trumpets and vials. Returning to these chapters adds much to the prophetic value of the Revelation.

Retrospective Chapters

It is necessary at this point to review the chapters of the Revelation between the sixth trumpet and the first vial. These chapters are placed in the scroll at the time that historians recognize as the great divide between the Middle Ages and the modern era. It is the appropriate place in the prophecy for insights into complex events passed over during the signal events of the trumpet eras. These chapters are written on the reverse side of the scroll, adding details that verify the historic meaning of the text.[18]

The Little Book (Chapter 10) – the New Testament
Verse 8

> *And the voice I heard from heaven spake unto me again, and said, Go and take the little book which is open in the hand of the angel which standeth upon the sea and upon the earth.*

---

18   Revelation, chapter 5, verse 1: "… a book [scroll] written within and on the back side, sealed with seven seals."

Verse 10

> *And I took the little book out of the angel's hand, and*
> *ate it up; and it was in my mouth sweet as honey; and as*
> *soon as I had eaten it, my belly was bitter.*

The little book refers to the New Testament, which became available to the common man with the translations from Latin into German, by Martin Luther, and English, by William Tyndale. These translations in the 1520s were joyfully accepted by people who had no real knowledge of Christianity due to the proclamations of the papacy that reading the Bible in a common language was a sin. Fortunately, the printing press had been invented around 1450, and it was put to good use by Protestants. However, the sweet taste of the Bible turned into bitterness when various Protestant churches argued among themselves, leading to the denominations of today's churches.

Two Witnesses of God (Chapter 11) – the living Bible

Chapter 11, verse 1

> *And there was given unto me a reed like unto a rod: and*
> *the angel stood, saying, Rise, and measure the temple of*
> *God and the altar, and them that worship therein.*

Verse 2

> *But the court which is without the temple leave out,*
> *and measure it not; for it is given unto the Gentiles: and*
> *the holy city shall they tread under foot forty and two*
> *months.*

In 380 A.D., Christianity became the official religion of the Roman Empire. A great flood of pagans entered into the churches without any experience of a spiritual encounter with Christ. These are the Gentiles who do not set their lives on

God's altar. They form a large part of Christianity, even today, during the Laodecian church age of indifference.

Forty-two months are 1260 years, Biblically. Added to 380 A.D., it leads to 1640 A.D., which is the time in history when Christianity began to return to the spiritual experience of Christ. This effort by individuals to experience grace, faith and salvation has come to be called the Pietist Movement. Various small groups and persons led the way out of mere memberships in state churches toward a life of spiritual rebirth in churches independent of governments.

In England, the Pietist Movement became the Quaker church led by George Fox, beginning in 1647. They believed every human being could realize their "inner light" as a witness to the reality of God. In Europe, after the murder of thousands of Anabaptist Christians in the 16th century, the movement of people to a personal and independent Christianity was carried forward to the evangelical movement of the 18th century. Looking back from our place in history, it seems reasonable to assign 1260 years—from 380 to 1640 A.D.—as a time when gentiles "tread underfoot" an intimate form of Christianity.

Verse 3

> *And I will give power unto my two witnesses, and they shall prophesy a thousand two hundred and three score days, clothed in sackcloth.*

The two witnesses are the two testaments—covenants between God and man—that are the Bible. It can be understood that they are alive in God's spirit. Historically, we are aware of the first compilation of the New Testament list of books about 190 A.D.[19] Adding 1260 years, we have a date

19   Known as the *Muratorian Canon.*

of 1450 A.D., which coincides with the first printed Bibles. During much of this long period of time, the Bible was not well used by most Christians. Dressed in the sackcloth of mourning is an expression of limited use. The common people and many priests could not read Latin, and ceremony replaced knowledge. Reading the Bible in any other language was a sin according to the Roman Catholic Church. This resulted in the passive obedience of Catholics regarding the Christian religion. The priestly catechism replaced the Bible.

Verse 7

> *And when they shall have finished their testimony, the beast that ascendeth out of the bottomless pit shall make war against them, and shall overcome them, and kill them.*

The beast refers to the Holy Roman Empire, the political and religious authority of the Middle Ages. In 1521 A.D., Luther was excommunicated and made his defense before the Imperial Diet based on the Bible, rejecting the long tradition of papal authority to rule Christ's church. Hiding from emperor and Pope, Luther translated the Bible into German. At the same time, William Tyndale translated the Bible into English. The two witnesses of the Old and New Testaments of the Bible rose from the dead, so to speak, with the publication and popularity of these Bibles—about 1525-1526 A.D. The Bible of the Protestants became the defining authority of God, supplanting Catholic appeals to their own traditions of papal authority.

Verse 13

> *And the same hour was there a great earthquake, and the tenth part of the city fell, and in the earthquake were slain of men seven thousand: and the remnant were affrighted, and gave glory to the God of heaven.*

This verse clarifies the identity of the witnesses, and the time of their being raised up to heaven. During the time when the Bible was being translated into common languages, it was being burned in the streets by Roman Catholic priests. At almost the same time, the Holy Roman Empire erupted into Protestant and Catholic kingdoms, becoming the religious "earthquake" of Christendom. In May 1527, the army of the Holy Roman Empire—the beast of Revelation—entered Rome, plundered the city and churches, killed many, and ridiculed the captured Pope.[20] This famous Sack of Rome was so traumatic to the Catholic Church that some attention was given to reforming itself when the Pope began a weak reform effort in 1536.

Verse 14

> *The second woe is past; and behold, the third woe cometh quickly.*

It will be recalled that the first woe described the "locusts" of the Arab Muslims. The second woe described the "horsemen" of the Turkish Muslims. The remaining portion of this chapter looks forward to the third and last woe—from the Reformation to today.

A Woman Gives Birth to a Son (Chapter 12)

This chapter describes a heavenly woman who gives birth to a human child who is to rule all nations. Some believe the woman represents Israel, and others believe she represents the Church of Christ. Another wonder of heaven is described as a red dragon having seven heads and ten horns with crowns. This dragon is identified as Satan, who is thrown down to

---

20   Some historians estimate 8,000 killed. Revelation's 7,000 is reasonable.

earth to try to devour the woman and those who overcome Satan with the blood sacrifice of Christ. The dragon casts out of his mouth a flood to drown the woman, meaning the influx of pagans around 380 A.D. into Christianity. These former pagans did not seek the deep spiritual effort of Christianity, and transferred much of the pagan religions to Christian beliefs and practices.

The woman escapes to the wilderness for 1260 years, which suggests the timing of the early missionary movement of British origin to the end of the religious wars of the Reformation. It was the Celtic and Anglo-Saxon monks who took Christianity to much of northern Europe during the Dark Ages. At that time, Ireland and Scotland were so remote to Rome that their religion resembled the earlier ideals of Christianity.

The Wild Animal (Chapter 13) – the Holy Roman Empire

The beast of this chapter describes the rise of the barbarian tribes who eventually became the Holy Roman Empire of the Middle Ages. This beast of the Revelation follows from the visions of the prophet Daniel of the Old Testament. It is difficult to hold these images in mind, and the following summary may help the reader through the first ten verses.

> *The dragon = the Satanic source of the seven imperial powers*
>
> *The seven heads = the seven Biblical empires in historical order: Egyptian, Assyrian, Babylonian, Persian, Grecian, Roman (to 476 A.D.), and the wounded but revived Roman Empire of Justinian in the 6th century*
>
> *The eighth head = The weak Holy Roman Empire that developed slowly from the Barbarian tribes and ended in 1806 A.D.*

All of these heads shared the characteristics of worldly empires whose leaders believed themselves approved by God.

These are followed by a different beast with special powers. This beast with the small horns attracts our greatest interest.

Verse 11

> *And I beheld another beast coming up out of the earth; and he had two horns like a lamb, and he spake as a dragon.*

Verse 12

> *And he exerciseth all the power of the first beast before him, and causeth the earth and them that dwell therein to worship the first beast whose deadly wound was healed.*

As the papacy developed, it claimed a spiritual authority over the kings and emperors of Europe. However, it supported the political power of these rulers—the eventual Holy Roman Empire in particular. The papal bureaucracy was modeled after the Roman Empire—the previous beast. The Holy Roman Empire and the Roman Catholic Church were one and the same thing in their ambition for wealth and power. They were honored because they were believed to have been ordained by God.

Verse 13

> *And he doeth great wonders, so that he maketh fire come down from heaven on earth in the sight of men.*

The phrase "in the sight of men" means that people will believe that this lamb-beast has God's authority to punish people. It was believed that the Popes could doom a person to hell's fire by excommunication. This pretense of God's authority was a fiction that was used to control kings and dissenters for many centuries.

The Popes of the 11th century into modern times believed themselves the head of God's authority on earth, with kings and emperors being the political or secular servants of the Pope. Thousands were killed in papal wars and the trials of the Inquisition to maintain this fiction, or "image," of the beast of papal government.

Verse 16

> *And he causeth all, both small and great, rich and poor, free and bond, to receive a mark in their right hand, or in their foreheads:*

The "right hand" refers to one's occupation. The mark on the "forehead" refers to one's beliefs.

Verse 17

> *And that no man may buy or sell, save he that had the mark, or the name of the beast, or the number of his name.*

When reviewing history, it is easy to forget the ordinary activities of commerce. The Middle Ages of Europe had a top to bottom marketing system of local monopolies. The kings made grants to individuals called guild merchants, who had trading rights for a town, with authority to exclude others. Within towns, there were craft guilds for every sort of occupation of hands or mind. These were also bound to their trade, and blessed in their occupations by the local priests. The local king and his lords received their right to rule based on the theory that the Pope, with God's authority, crowned kings or emperors. Papal edicts commanded that no one was to buy or sell without the approval of the church.[21] It was a highly restrictive system.

---

21   For example, the Third Lateran Council of 1178 A.D, the Fourth Lateran Council of 1215 A.D., and the Council of Constance of 1417 A.D.

Verse 18

> *Here is wisdom. Let him that hath understanding count*
> *the number of the beast: for it is the number of a man;*
> *and his number is six hundred threescore and six.*

The Latin language of the Papacy uses letters of the alphabet to compute numbers. The number 666 adds from the inscription on the crown of gold placed upon the head of the Pope at his coronation. It reads *VICARIUS FELII DEI* which translates as Vicar (stand-in for) the Son of God. V(5) I (1) C (100) ARI (1) U (5) S FI (1) L(50) I (1) I (1) D (500) EI (1) which totals to 666. Of course, no one can assume the authority of Christ.

VICARIUS FILII DEI

This translates as Vicar (stand in for) the Son of God.

V	5	F		D	500
I	1	I	1	E	
C	100	L	50	I	1
A		I	1		
R		I	1		
I	1				
U	5				
S					
	112	+	53	+	501 = 666

In Matthew Chapter 16, verse 19, concerning what Jesus tells Peter, the correct translation from the original Greek is "what he [Peter] binds on earth" will be "what has been bound" [by God] in Heaven – not as the papacy promotes as permission for the popes to define and forgive sins with God's authority.[22]

It may be noted here that the term "Antichrist" also means one who is the stand-in for Christ, as well as one who opposes Christ. It means exactly the same thing in Greek as in Latin.

The Harvest of the Earth (Chapter 14) – the Gospel preached

This chapter deals with the spread of Christianity, beginning with the 144,000 missionary monks of the early centuries, who are redeemed from mankind as the first fruits of the great harvest. It then pictures the spread of the Gospel throughout the world. The number 144,000 reminds us of the twelve apostles times 12,000.

Verse 6

> And I saw another angel fly in the midst of heaven (mid-heaven), having the everlasting gospel to preach unto them that dwell on the earth, and to every nation, and kindred, and tongue and people.

This Gospel proclamation to the whole world from mid-heaven occurs with the radio and television broadcasting that has resulted in millions of new Christians. Other verses give dire warnings to those who worship the beast and his image, and receive his mark in their forehead, or hand, indicating their beliefs or actions.

---

22 Marshall, Alfred, *The R.S.V. Interlinear Greek-English New Testament,* p. iii and p. 71, Zondervan, 1968

The concluding verses describe God's anger with the harvest of the blood of Christians that flows for "the space of 1600 furlongs." This description of the winepress of God's anger probably refers to time, and the 1,600 years from 48 A.D. and the first martyrs, to 1648 A.D. and the end of the religious wars. It is a cryptic statement of time because 1,600 years would have been too discouraging in earlier centuries.

THE GREAT WHORE (Chapter 17) – Papal Rome

Chapter 17 is a description of the religious organization of Babylon, called the great whore. Since the Reformation of the 16th century, all of the Protestant churches recognized the papacy in this chapter, but it is seldom discussed today.

Verse 1

Come hither; I will show onto thee the judgment of the great whore…

Verse 2

With whom the kings of the [Roman] earth have committed fornication…

Fornication is the biblical reference to idolatry, and the mixing of pagan practices with Christianity.

Verse 3

…and I saw a woman sit upon a scarlet-colored beast, full of names of blasphemy, having seven heads and ten horns.

Verse 4

And the woman was arrayed in purple and scarlet color, and decked with gold and precious stones and pearls, having a golden cup in her hand full of abominations…

Verse 6

> *And I saw the woman drunken with the blood of saints,*
> *and with the blood of the martyrs of Jesus*

It is one of the great ironies of history that those who claimed control of the Christian people reveled in the torture and the murder of thousands of Christians from the 12th through 17th century.

Verse 9

> *And here is the mind which has wisdom. The seven heads*
> *are seven mountains, on which the woman sitteth.*

The seven hills of Rome identify the papacy as the great whore. The seven mountains also allude to the great empires of the Biblical world, all claiming God's authority to rule.

Verse 10

> *And there are seven kings: five are fallen, and one is, and*
> *the other is not yet come; and when he cometh, he must*
> *continue a short space.*

The seven biblical empires are, beginning in the 10th century B.C.:

1. Egyptian
2. Assyrian
3. Babylonian
4. Persian
5. Greek
6. Roman—existing when the Revelation was written, and
7. The revived Roman Empire of the 6th century.

When the Emperor Justinian came to power in 527 A.D., almost all of the Roman Empire west of Constantinople had been overrun by various barbarian tribes. When he died in

565 A.D., almost all of the old Roman Empire had been reconstituted by defeating the Vandals in North Africa and the Goths in Italy. This astonishing healing of the wounded head was short-lived, however. The Lombard victories in Italy in 568 A.D. might be seen as the beginning of the Dark Ages of medieval history.

Verse 16

> *And the ten horns that thou sawest upon the beast, those shall hate the whore, and shall make her desolate and naked, and shall eat her flesh, and burn her with fire.*

The ten horns symbolically refer to the Barbarian tribes that eventually became the Holy Roman Empire, with ten electors (later seven) choosing the Emperor. The Empire and the papacy were frequently in conflict with each other.

The Roman version of Christianity became perverted by combining pagan mystery religions with the pure faith of the first three centuries of Christianity. The worship of Mary was firmly established by the 5th century, following pagan worship of female deities. In place of the intimate quest of early Christians for communion with God in Christ, the Roman priesthood taught devotion to ceremonies and relics, while denying the average person access to the Bible. Those who searched for spiritual truth outside of the church hierarchy were subjected to the gruesome tortures of the Inquisition. Thousands of good people were murdered from the 12th to 18th centuries—with priestly enthusiasm. Modern histories slide over the horrific history of the Roman church.

Also passed over is the historic fulfillment of this chapter of Revelation. This incident occurred in 1527 when German imperial soldiers, enflamed by Martin Luther's rejection of the papacy, destroyed much of Rome in a famous event known as the "sack of Rome." The destruction was much worse than that of the Vandals of the 5th century. Church property—altars, monasteries, and convents—were destroyed and burned. This attack provoked the attempted reforms of Catholicism which followed, but these reforms were used to continue the power of the papacy.

BABYLON AND BAGHDAD (Chapter 18)

Chapter 18 of the Revelation details the destruction of a city with the symbolic name of Babylon. Unfortunately, many commentators assume that this chapter refers to the future destruction of Rome and the papacy. However there are two Babylons that receive an historic destruction. One is the Sack of Rome in 1527 A.D.; the other is the downfall of the Arab Caliphate of Baghdad in 1258 A.D. The title of "Babylon" is used for both because it is the Biblical term for a false religion. It has its historic reference in 587 B.C. when the Jews were taken captive to Babylon. Ancient Babylon was abandoned in 275 B.C., and its ruins lie 45 miles south of modern Baghdad. Few readers of this chapter of the Revelation seem to be aware of the history of the original Baghdad or its spiritual significance as the Babylon of Islam.

The original Baghdad was established in 762 A.D. as a site for the Caliphate, the political, economic, and religious authority of the Muslim religion. Modern Baghdad is sited differently than the original city. The original Baghdad became the richest city in the world and a large, inland seaport, with hundreds of sailing ships docked for miles on the banks of the Tigris River.[23] These merchant ships came from India and Africa. Baghdad was also the destination of the merchant caravans drawn to the wealth of its markets. The Caliphs lost their personal power, but their spiritual significance was a central belief of the majority of Muslims. In some ways their spiritual significance can be compared to that of the popes. It must be understood that the Muslim religion is grounded in the belief that Muhammed is superior to Jesus, and that Jesus Christ is not from God, or a savior of mankind. The destruction of the original city of Baghdad in 1258 A.D. fits the description in Revelation. It was the end of the Arab Muslim empire.

The grandson of Ghenghiz Khan, Hulagu, came to Baghdad in 1258 A.D. with his army of Mongolian and Turkic cavalry with the intention of destruction and slaughter. This he accomplished with such relish that at least 80,000 were killed, including the Caliph, whom he rolled into a rug and beat to death. Almost no building was left standing. The city burned for weeks, and Hulagu ordered the elaborate canal system and the city plowed over. The apparent site of old Baghdad does not appear to have been rebuilt.

Baghdad became a small, poor, provincial city built on the eastern bank of the Tigris River. In 1914, the railroad was constructed on the western bank of the Tigris River, and modern Baghdad grew to its present size. It is notable, however, that a large area on the western side is uninhabited; some of it is an old military airport. Louis Massignon, writing

---

23   Payne, Robert, *The History of Islam*, Dorset Press, 1959, pp. 163, 239, 241.

in 1963, states that the center of old Baghdad—the Round City of 762 A.D. to 1258 A.D.—"...is now covered by a low, badly cultivated plain, full of ravines and deformed by floods, on the right bank between old Karkh to the east and the tombs of the two Shi-ite imams in Kazimain, to the northwest."[24] The Revelation states that this city will not be rebuilt, and we must remember that the descriptive details of this city and its destruction are historically unique.

Verse 4

...Babylon the great is fallen...

Verse 5

...Come out of her, my people...

Verse 9

And the kings of the earth, who have committed adultery with her and shared her luxury, see the smoke of her burning, they will weep and mourn over her.

Verse 10

Standing far off for the fear of her torment, saying 'Woe, woe, O great city, that great city Babylon, that mighty city, for in one hour thy judgment has come.'

Verse 11

and the merchants of the earth shall weep and mourn over her; for no one buyeth their merchandise any more

Verse 17

...and every shipmaster and all the company in ships, and sailors, and as many as trade by sea and stood afar off.

Verse 18

and cried when they saw the smoke of her burning...

---

24   Wiet, Gaston, *Baghdad*, University of Oklahoma Press, 1971, pp. 168-169.

Verse 22

> *and the voice of harpers, and musicians, and of pipers,*
> *and trumpeters shall be heard no more at all in thee…*

Verse 23

> *…for by thy sorceries were all nations deceived.*

Verse 27

> *and in her was found the blood of prophets and of saints*
> *and all that were slain [spiritually] upon the earth.*

The Caliphate was continued in a symbolic and powerless manner in Egypt until 1517. It was then assumed by the Sultans of the Turkish Ottoman Empire in Istanbul. It was formally abolished by the Turkish government in 1924, but God gave His judgment in 1258 A.D. No other destruction of a seaport city compares in all details and significance to the destruction of Baghdad.

THE NEAR FUTURE

Our greatest concern is for the events of the near future. After the seventh vial of World War II, the next Revelation events are heavenly scenes of the gathering up to heaven of worthy Christians; celestial warfare; a thousand year reign of Christ, and the final rebellion and judgment of all. The Bible gives us help to know when these events may begin.

The Final Jewish War

Several Old Testament prophets speak of a final war around Jerusalem. "Ezekiel" (Chapters 38 and 39) and "Zechariah" (Chapters 12, 13 and 14) are notable as scenes of a conclusive war for the Jewish people.

Zechariah 14 verse 12 (NIV)

> *This is the plague with which the Lord will strike all the nations that fought against Jerusalem. Their flesh will rot while they are still standing on their feet, their eyes will rot in their sockets, and their tongues will rot in their mouths.*

These wounds are unique to a war involving radioactive weapons, as was seen in Hiroshima's dying population in 1945.

Zechariah 12 verse 10 (NIV)

> *And I will pour out on the house of David and the inhabitants of Jerusalem a spirit of grace and supplication. They will look to me, the one they have pierced, and they will mourn for him, as one mourns for an only child, and grieve bitterly for him as one grieves for a first born son.*

There is much to learn from the prophets about the war for Jerusalem that is likely to occur in the near future. The point being that the use of a modern weapon, and the Jewish recognition of Jesus as their Messiah is consistent with a near date for these prophecies.

A near date for this final war seems plausible given the current political problems facing Israel today. Thousands of rockets have been brought into Lebanon by Iranian supported fighters sworn to attack Israel. Syria supports these efforts. With Iran gaining nuclear capabilities, and Turkey becoming hostile to Israel, it seems likely that a major disaster will occur before 2020. This war is prophetically separate from the Armageddon of World War II. It will be a war localized to Israel, including the plain of Megiddo.

Daniel's End-Time

Every generation of Christians has hoped that it would witness the end of tribulation and the beginning of the 1,000-year reign of Christ promises at the close of Revelation. Many bad guesses have been made. However, we are warned often in the New Testament that we are to live with the expectation of Christ's return. Furthermore, having reviewed the historic completion of the Revelation church ages, trumpet events, and signal vials, we come closer to an endpoint than any previous generation. We cannot know the exact time of Christ's return, but we are led to compute a time near that end by the last verses given to the prophet Daniel.

These final verses of Daniel's prophecy are the only Biblical statement of an end-time. Daniel's prophesies are complex and have been misunderstood. However, it is not necessary to explain the preceding visions in order to solve the puzzle of an end-time. If we understand that the last verses apply to the whole of Daniel's visions, as seems the most logical purpose of these verses, then we may solve the puzzle, given the historical span of time necessary for its solution. Clearly, Daniel is himself exasperated, and he wants a final date.

Daniel, Chapter 12, verse 8 New International Version

> *And I heard, but I understand not: then said I, O my Lord, what shall be the end of these things?*

Verse 9

> *And he said, Go thy way, Daniel: for the words are closed up and sealed till the time of the end.*

It is notable that we are told here that these words will be understood at the end-time.

Verse 10

> *Many shall be purified, and made white and tried, but the wicked shall do wickedly: and none of the wicked shall understand; but the wise shall understand.*

Verse 11

> *And from the time that the daily sacrifice shall be taken away, and the abomination that maketh desolate set*

up, there shall be a thousand two hundred and ninety days.

The use of the future tense "shall be" is unfortunate in this translation. The translation made by the renowned Daniel scholar, Edward J. Young is better:

And from the time of the turning aside of the continual [daily sacrifice] and to the giving of an abomination desolating is one thousand, two hundred and ninety days.[25]

Verse 12

Blessed is the one who waits for and reaches the end of the 1335 days.

The angel provides Daniel a starting point for a span of time from which to count 1,290 days – meaning prophetic years, as explained previously. For this span of time to be meaningful to Daniel, it must refer to an event within his lifetime. The first chapter of Daniel's prophecy tells of Daniel being sent as a captive to Babylon in his youth in 605 B.C.[26] At that time, Daniel witnessed the removal of sacred articles from the Jewish Temple, and the deposit of those articles in the Babylonian's temple. We can understand that the Babylonian's desired to remove the power of an avenging Jewish God to their own temple. The loss of the sacred articles used during the daily sacrifice marks the beginning of the calculation of 1,290 years – concluded in 686 A.D. with the construction of an abomination with a desolating result. The Hebrew indicates the construction of some object – not a man.

---

25   Young, Edward J., Th.M.Ph.D., *The Prophecy of Daniel*, Wm. B. Erdmans Publishing Co., Grand Rapids, Michigan, p. 261.

26   Finegan, Jack. *Handbook of Biblical Chronology*, revised edition, p. 254. Hendrickson Publishers, Box 3473, Peabody, MA 01961-3473

Between 686 A.D. and 692 A.D., the Muslim shrine of the Dome of the Rock was built on the temple mount in Jerusalem to honor the Muslim belief that Muhammed dreamed of rising to heaven from the "distant mountain." The purpose of this shrine is to declare Muhammed superior to Jesus Christ, and to deny His divinity. It is the only monumental insult to God ever constructed. It is an abomination with a desolating significance for one third of the world's people who are denied the truth of Christ. The inscription around the inside of the Dome of the Rock has a mocking tone:

"So believe in God and all the messengers, and stop talking about a Trinity. Cease in your own best interests! Verily God is the God of unity, Lord Almighty! That God would beget a child? Either in the Heavens or on the Earth?"[27]

Over a gate is a plate inscribed: "The Sonship of Jesus and the Trinity are false."[28]

The existence of this shrine in Jerusalem is the basis for the Muslim wars with Israel that threaten world peace today. It is the Muslim declaration of their claim to Jerusalem.

The second step in the angel's riddle to Daniel is the addition of 1,335 more years to the end-time. Therefore, 686/7 A.D. plus 1,335 years brings us to ca. 2021 A.D. This may be the approximate time when Christ gathers his faithful believers, or when the 1,000 years of Christ's return will begin.

---

27 Nuseibeh, Said and Grabar, Oleg, The Dome of the Rock. See also Biblical Archaeology Review, July/August 2006, "Islam on the Temple Mount," p.45.

28 Ibid; p.42.

Conclusion

It is amazing that the Revelation can be understood as a symbolic sketch of 1900 years of Christendom. Unfortunately, televangelists and popular writers have misunderstood the Revelation, and have conflated several other Biblical prophecies with the Revelation. This misunderstanding creates an imagined future of invading Russian and Chinese armies, and a satanic world dictator. This has the effect of making Christianity seem foolish to the unbeliever. Hopefully, understanding the Revelation correctly will help some to realize that Christ is indeed one with God, and that He will return in some way to establish His heavenly kingdom very soon.

It seems likely that some of the identifications made in this commentary will cause difficulty for some readers. Nevertheless, there are many more identifications where the prophecy and history are almost obvious. The prophetic verses are like steppingstones across the river of Christian history. Enough is given in the great scope of this vision to assure us that God is in Christ, and that Christ is our Savior.

We may soon expect the celestial sign of His return, which will be seen from horizon to horizon, as promised in Mathew 24, verses 30:

> *And then shall appear the sign of the Son of Man in heaven: and then shall all of the tribes of the earth mourn, and they shall see the Son of Man coming in the clouds of heaven with power and great glory.*

This sign may involve Venus as Christ calls Himself "the bright Morning Star" at the close of the Revelation. This event will probably occur after the Jewish war, but it would be unwise to wait for an event or sign before believing in Christ's salvation. Although the intellectual evidence for His deity approaches certainty in fulfilled prophecies, only the heart provides the way to His companionship.

Additional Sources

Bryce, James, *The Holy Roman Empire*, Schocken Books, New York, 1961.

Campbell, Alan, many helpful booklets, Open Bible Ministries, P.O. Box 92, Belfast, BT5 7SA, North Ireland

Covenant Publishing Co., booklist, P.O. Box 534, Rose Bud, Arkansas 72137-0534

Fox, John S., *A Flood of Light UPON THE BOOK OF REVELATION,* The Association of the Covenant People, P.O. Box 1478, Ferndale, WA 98248

Foster, Thomas, *Amazing Book of Revelation Explained!* Crusade Centre, Kingdom Digest, Box 24600, Dallas, Texas 75224, 1984.

Frankforter, A. Daniel, *A History of the Christian Movement*, Nelson-Hall, Chicago, 1978

Heer, Friedrich, *The Medieval World Europe 1100 – 1350*, 1961, Phoenix, Orion House, 5 Upper St. Martins Lane, London, WC2H 9EA, 1998 reprint

Hunt, Dave, *A Woman Rides the Beast*, Harvest House Publishers, Eugene, Oregon 97402. A Protestant view of the Roman Catholic Church.

Moss, H. St. L. B., *The Birth of the Middle Ages, 395-814 A.D.*, Oxford University Press, 1935.

Rendina, Claudio, *The Popes, Histories and Secrets,* Seven Locks Press, P.O. Box 25689, Santa Ana, CA 92799, 2002.

Shelly, Bruce L., *Church History in Plain Language*, Word Books, 4800 West Waco Dr., Waco, Texas 76703, 1982

Stearns, Peter N., editor, *The Encyclopedia of World History*, Houghton Mifflin Co., 2001